CHIEF WAPELLO

The Man, The Leader, The Statue

Leigh Michaels
Michael W. Lemberger

PBL Limited
Ottumwa Iowa

Chief Wapello: The Man, The Leader, The Statue
Copyright 2014 by Leigh Michaels & Michael W. Lemberger

Cover and design copyright 2014 by Michael W. Lemberger

This edition published 2014

10 9 8 7 6 5 4 3 2 1

ISBN 1892689936
ISBN 13: 9781892689931

Printed in the United States of America

Illustrations courtesy of **The Lemberger Collection**. For more information about the collection, which has been called the largest and best-documented privately-owned photography collection in the world, visit www.mlemberger.com.

All rights reserved. Except for brief passages quoted in any review, the reproduction or utilization of this work in whole or in part, in any form or by any electronic, mechanical, or other means, now known or hereinafter invented, including xerography, photocopying and recording, or in any information storage and retrieval system, is forbidden without the express permission of the publisher. For permission contact:
    Rights Editor
    PBL Limited
    P.O. Box 935
    Ottumwa IA 52501-0935
    pbl@pbllimited.com

Visit our website at www.pbllimited.com for more information about this and other publications. Quantity and wholesale prices are available.

CHIEF WAPELLO

The Man, The Leader, The Statue

CHIEF WAPELLO

Statue atop the Wapello County Courthouse in February 1968.

CHIEF WAPELLO

When we first mentioned writing a book about Chief Wapello, people asked, "Do you mean the man, or the statue?"

It's a good question because the two are definitely not the same. The Native American statue atop the Wapello County Courthouse is an iconic image, but it is not based on the historic chief of the Sac and Fox tribes who made his home near Ottumwa. A noted pacifist, Wapello is not known to have ever sported the sort of war bonnet which the statue wears; in fact, the statue's feathered bonnet is more typical of Sioux Indians, traditionally a foe of the Sac and Fox.

Little is known about the historic Chief Wapello; the unembellished details can easily fit on a single page. Not much more is known about the statue -- the sculptor is nameless, as are the details of how this particular figure was chosen from the pages of an architectural catalog.

And yet this statue and the person it has long represented are much more than the namesake of an Iowa county. When a storm blew the statue down from its courthouse perch in 2012, crowds gathered to watch with breath held until the chief was lifted from his precarious resting place to safety. And when, restored to glory, he was returned to his pedestal overlooking the Des Moines River valley in March 2014, crowds applauded.

Our goal is to assemble in one volume what is known about Chief Wapello -- the man, the leader, and the statue which is affectionately called by his name. The story spans more than two centuries, from the birth of a Native American boy in what would become Wisconsin to the day the restored statue was returned to the top of the Wapello County Courthouse.

Much of the text in this book is quoted from various histories of Wapello County and of the Sac and Fox tribes. We have tried to find the sources closest to the events, but dates are sometimes uncertain, authors sometimes disagree, and in some cases multiple versions have been published. To maintain the readability of the text, identifying labels have been used with the quoted text rather than employing detailed footnotes. Complete information regarding sources is on page 85.

We wish to thank the Wapello County Supervisors (Greg Kenning, Jerry Parker, and Steve Siegel) for their assistance, Phyllis Dean for sharing her records of the courthouse construction and early days of county government, Pat Myers for her assistance with research, the Wapello County Historical Musem for sharing maps and resources, and Cheryl Cox for proofreading the text.

---Michael W. Lemberger & Leigh Michaels

TIMELINE

1787 -- Wapello is born at Prairie du Chien, Northwest Territory (later Wisconsin)

1803 -- Louisiana Purchase transfers title of the area which became Wapello County from France to the United States.

1812 -- The State of Louisiana is admitted into the Union, and the country north of it is renamed Missouri Territory.

1833 -- A treaty with the Sac and Fox tribe of Indians tranfers a section of Iowa lying west of the Mississippi River and east of the west line of Jefferson county to the United States.

1834 -- The land which is now Iowa becomes part of Michigan Territory.

1837 -- The State of Michigan is admitted to the Union, and the country west of Michigan is renamed Wisconsin Territory.

1837 -- A party of chiefs (including Wapello, Keokuk, and Appanoose) travels to Washington D.C. and other eastern cities.

1838 -- Iowa is organized as a separate territory.

1838 -- A new Indian Agency is established by General Joseph M. Street on the Des Moines River to serve the Sac and Fox Indians.

1840 -- General Street dies at the Indian Agency and, at the request of the Sac and Fox Indians, is buried in the Agency gardens.

1842 -- (March 15) While hunting along the Skunk River, Wapello is taken ill and dies and, at his own request, is buried next to his friend General Street.

1842 -- (October 11) A treaty with the Sac and Fox tribes cedes the remainder of Iowa to the United States for a total of $800,000, or about 12 cents per acre.

1843 -- (May 1) First legal settlement begins in the newly-ceded area (including Wapello County) by whites.

1843 -- (February 17) Wapello County is established.

1844 -- Ottumwa is established.

1846 -- The State of Iowa is admitted to the Union.

1894 -- Wapello County Courthouse is dedicated.

1901 -- C B & Q Railroad acquires title to the gravesite, along with land just south of the site in order to relocate railroad tracks.

1901-1903 -- C B & Q erects white picket fence enclosure of the graves.

1912 -- Agency House is torn down.

1929-30 -- Burlington Railroad spends $1,200 to create a park around the graves, including a raised mound carrying the name for the benefit of passengers on passing trains. A white metal obelisk and a new black fence are erected.

After 1939 -- Capstones on the graves of General and Mrs. Street are replaced.

1946 -- As part of Iowa's centennial-year celebration, the park is improved with new fencing and the placement of a boulder and bronze plate marking the site of the Agency House.

Statue atop the Wapello County Courthouse,
taken from the courthouse roof, October 28, 1974.

1951 -- A glacial boulder and bronze plaque commemorating the treaty which transferred ownership of Iowa and the first Christian service held in the interior of Iowa is placed at the gravesite.
1965 -- A stainless steel obelisk replaces the metal one erected in 1929.
1975 -- Chief Wapello Memorial Park is listed on the National Register of Historic Places.
1976 -- Title to the Chief Wapello Memorial Park is turned over from the Burlington Northern Railroad to the Chief Wapello Memorial Park Association. The graves are more securely fenced and roofed for protection, and a kiosk is added to give history and background to the park.
1987 -- New park displays and enclosures are built.
1990 -- "Chief Wapello" letters are set in concrete; park landscaping is added.

WAPELLO

"The name Wapello signifies *prince* or *chief*. He was head chief of the Fox tribe, and was born at Prairie du Chien in 1787. At the time of the erection of Fort Armstrong (1816) he presided over one of the three principal villages in that vicinity. His village was on the east side of the Mississippi, near the foot of Rock Island, and not far from the famous Black Hawk village.

In 1829 he removed his village to Muscatine Slough, on the west side of the Mississippi, and then to a place at or near the present town of Wapello, in Louisa county. Like Keokuk and Pashepaho, he was in favor of abiding by the requirements of the treaty of 1804, and was therefore opposed to the hostile movements of Black Hawk.

Wapello was among the chiefs present on the occasion of the liberation of Black Hawk at Fort Armstrong, in 1833. At that time, after several chiefs had spoken, he rose in the council and said 'I am not in the habit of talking – *I think*. I have been thinking all day; Keokuk has spoken; I am glad to see my brothers; I will shake hands with them. I am done.'

The name of Wapello appears signed to several treaties relinquishing lands to the United States. He was one of the delegates who accompanied Keokuk to Washington in 1837. On that occasion he made a very favorable impression by the correctness of his deportment. He made a speech in the council, which was held at that time by the secretary of war for the purpose of reconciling the Sioux with the Sacs and Foxes. After Keokuk had spoken Wapello commenced his speech by saying: 'My father, you have heard what my chief has said. He is the chief of our nation. His tongue is ours. What he says we all say. Whatever he does we will be bound by it.' It was conceded that Wapello's remarks were sensible and pertinent, and although he did not possess the fine form and commanding presence of Keokuk, many thought his speech was not inferior to Keokuk's.

After the conclusion of the business at Washington, the delegation visited Boston, where they held a levee at Faneuil Hall, and were afterward conducted to the State-house, where they were received by Governor Everett, members of the legislature, and other dignitaries. The governor addressed them, and the chiefs replied, Keokuk, as usual, speaking first. He was followed by Wapello, who said: 'I am happy to meet my friends in the land of my forefathers. When a boy I recollect my grandfather told me of this place where the white men used to take our forefathers by the hand. I am very happy that this

---

Right: The only portrait of Chief Wapello known to have been painted from life. The artist was Charles Bird King, and the painting was made during Wapello's visit to Washington, D.C. in 1837. The turban and red-dyed locks of hair were typical Sac and Fox attire. (Courtesy Wapello County Historical Society)

The Lemberger Collection

WA-PEL-LA
CHIEF OF THE MUSQUAKEES.

land has induced so many white men to come upon it; by that I think they can get a living upon it... I am always glad to give the white man my hand, and call him brother. The white man is the older of the two; but perhaps you have heard that my tribe is respected by all others, and is the oldest among the tribes. I have shaken hands with a great many different tribes of people. I am very much gratified that I have lived to come and talk with the white man in this house, where my fathers talked, which I have heard of so many years ago. I will go home and tell all I have seen, and it shall never be forgotten by my children.' ...

In the spring of 1842, Wapello had left his village on the Des Moines, not far from the site of the present city of Ottumwa, to visit the grand scenes of his former hunting exploits. It was in March – the dreary moon of storms – but there were days when all nature seemed to rejoice at the near approach of the season of springing grass and budding leaves. Alas! the good chief had numbered his winters on earth. His moccasins were never again to press the green carpet of the prairies, nor follow the trail of the deer amid the coverts of the forest. While encamped with his hunting party on Rock Creek, in what is now Jackson township, Keokuk county, he was taken suddenly ill. Surrounded by his faithful followers, he lingered but a few days, and then on the 15th of March, 1842, his spirit passed away to the better hunting grounds. To the curious it may in the years to come be a matter of interest to know that the closing scene in the earthly career of this good Indian chief was on the northwest quarter of the northeast quarter of section twenty-one, township seventy-four, range eleven.

In accordance with a request made by Wapello some time before his death, his remains were conveyed to the agency for interment near those of General Street, the former beloved agent of the Sacs and Foxes. The funeral cortege accompanying the remains from the place of his death to the agency, consisted of Samuel Hardesty, and twenty-five Indians, three of whom were squaws. In the presence of Keokuk, Appanoose, and most of the leading men of the tribes, on the same evening of the arrival of the body, after the usual Indian ceremonies, the interment took place. Since then the remains of Wapello have peacefully reposed beside those of his pale-faced friend, and suitable monuments mark the resting place of both...."

-- FULTON

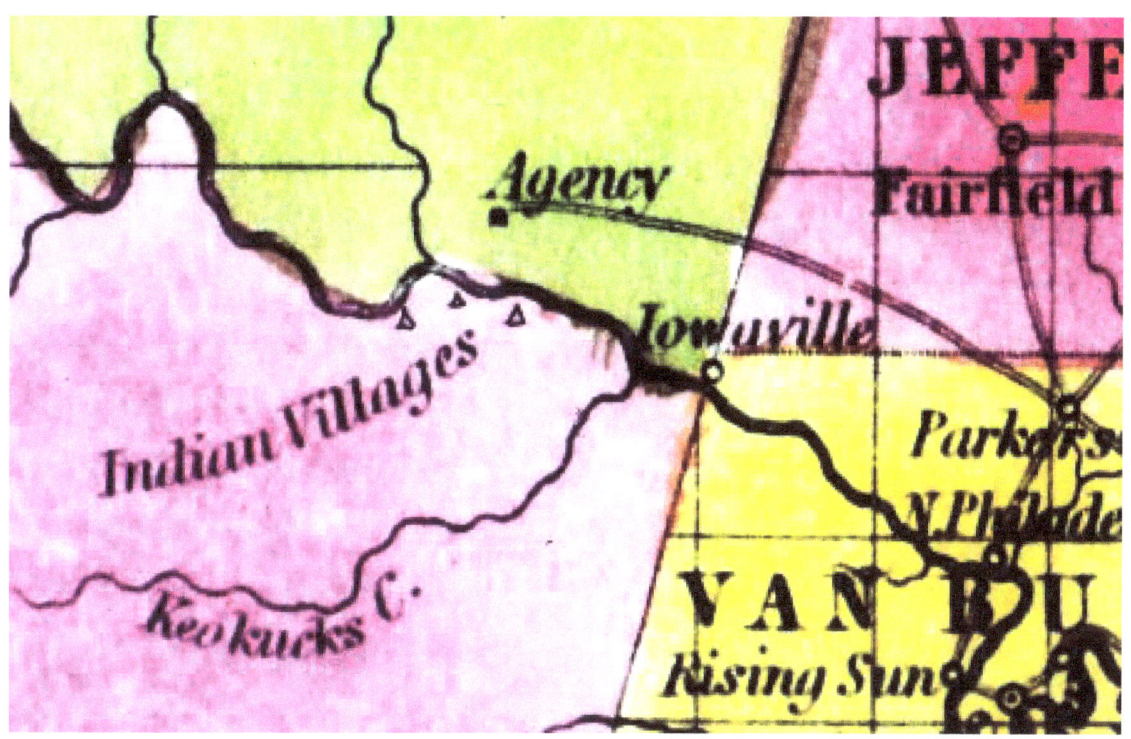

Section of an Iowa map printed in 1841, showing the relative positions of Indian villages along the Des Moines River to the Agency. The curves of the river at top left mark the current-day site of Ottumwa.

"The steps of organization, which led to the marking out of the boundaries of Wapello county, may be summarized as follows: Originally it was included in the Louisiana Purchase of 1803; in 1804 this territory was divided into the governments of Louisiana and Orleans. In 1812 Louisiana was admitted into the Union, and the country north of it was then called Missouri Territory. From 1812 to 1834 that region of country now embraced in Iowa was a part of Missouri Territory. In the latter year Iowa was placed under the jurisdiction of Michigan and was known as a part of Michigan Territory. In 1837 the state of Michigan was admitted to the Union, and this had led to the organization, in the previous year, of a new territory under the name of Wisconsin; Iowa was then a part of Wisconsin. Iowa was created as a separate territory in 1838. In 1833 a treaty was made with the Sac and Fox tribe of Indians, by the terms of which the country lying west of the Mississippi River and east of the west line of Jefferson county was ceded to the United States by the Indians. On the 11th of October, 1842, a second treaty was made with the same tribe, by which the remainder of Iowa was ceded. Under this latter treaty the whites were not permitted to settle within what are now the boundaries of Wapello county until the 1st of May, 1843."   -- EVANS

GENERAL JOSEPH M. STREET

"Gen. Joseph M. Street was born in Virginia, October 18, 1782. He was appointed to the agency of the Winnebagoes in 1828, and in the autumn of this year arrived at Prairie du Chien, his family remaining for a short time in Illinois. During the winter he returned and removed his family also to the agency. He was a strict Presbyterian, and his was the first family professing the Protestant faith to locate at that place.

After the treaty of 1837, by which the Sacs and Foxes relinquished 'Keokuk's Reserve' on the Iowa River, and the Indians agreed to remove further west, General Street was transferred from the agency at Prairie du Chien to the new agency of the Sacs and Foxes on the Des Moines. In accordance with this purpose, early in 1838 General Street took measures to locate a new agency as convenient as practicable to the principal villages of the Indians. Accompanied by the chief, Poweshiek, and a party of Indians, he set out to examine the country and selected the location, where the town of Agency City is now situated in Wapello county. He at once contracted for the erection of the necessary buildings, including a family residence and office, blacksmith shop and stables. The contractor was from Clarksville, Missouri; he brought with him a large force of mechanics and laborers, including a number of negro [sic] slaves. The work was soon completed....

In April, 1839, General Street removed his family to the new agency. In the meantime his health had been gradually declining, and before the close of the year he had become almost totally disabled, owing to a complication of obstinate maladies. On the 5th day of May, 1840, he was out riding with his brother-in-law, Dr. Posey, who had been attending him professionally. On returning home, he alighted from the carriage, and seating himself in the door, called for a cup of cold water. When the servant brought it, he remained motionless in the chair. Dr. Posey was immediately called, and came without the delay of a minute, but too late. The General had died while sitting in his chair."-- FULTON

In August 1838 "[t]he old council house, intended for a place wherein to hold talks with the Indians, was already completed, being the first building put up, with a view to using it as a shelter for the provisions and other perishable stores. Many of the timbers for the agency house were upon the ground and being continually hauled there, ready hewn. Two heavy breaking teams were at work upon the future field and wagons hauling the rails, and with the ring of the blacksmith's hammer quite a business air was imparted to the new settlement....

By winter the contract was about completed and the buildings ready for occupancy. In April, 1839, General Street moved down his family from Prairie du Chien and took possession. Ere long his health began to fail and the result was a combination of obstinate maladies under which he succumbed early in May of the next year....

The Indians were greatly attached to their "Father," as they usually term their agent, and word of the general's sudden demise reaching the villages opposite Ottumwa, numbers of them came immediately to the agency. Wapello and his band especially, were so demonstrative in their grief as to augment the distress of Mrs. Street ... it became necessary to have the interpreter kindly explain it to them and beg them to give expression to their sorrow at some point more remote from the house.

[Major Beach] ...hastened to Washington as soon as the sad news reached him, the hope being to save the family their home, in which they were now comfortably established, and of which the succession of a stranger to the office would have deprived them. When he arrived there, by a then unusually quick journey of twelve days, he found his nomination already awaiting the action of the Senate.... At the time of his arrival about June 1, 1840, the agency, with its dependencies, was about as follows: In the agency house was Mrs. Street and the nine youngest of her children... in the rear of the agency, was Josiah Smart, the interpreter.... and within a few steps of his residence was that of the blacksmith, Charles H. Withington. There was also Harry Sturdevant, the gunsmith, but being unmarried, he boarded with Withington until a year or so later he put himself up a cabin... Then there was the household of the Pattern Farm, some half-dozen in number... This was the actual agency settlement. On the Des Moines... where the bluff approaches nearest to the bank, was the trading post of P. Chouteau, Sr., & Company, but later more familiarly known as the "Old Garrison." This was usually superintended by Capt. William Phelps. And just above the mouth of Sugar Creek, on the creek bank, at the old road crossing, lived the miller, Jeremiah Smith, Jr., with his family. This embraced all the whites lawfully living in the country at the time."   -- WATERMAN

MAJOR JOHN BEACH

"Major John Beach, who succeeded General Street as Indian agent, was born at Gloucester, Massachusetts, February 23, 1812. At an early age he entered Portsmouth (N.H.) Academy, where at ten years of age he took a prize for proficiency in Latin, and at thirteen he excelled in Greek. He was appointed a cadet at West Point at the age of sixteen, and graduated in the class of 1832 at the age of twenty years. Soon after he received his commission as second lieutenant in the First U.S. Infantry, of which Zachary Taylor was colonel. He was assigned to duty on the frontier and in 1838, his hearing having become impaired, he resigned from the army and was for some time employed in the United States land office at Dubuque. In the meantime he had married a daughter of General Street, and succeeded him as agent in 1840. [*Editor's note:* After the Agency in Wapello County was closed, Beach served as agent in the new agency located at Fort Des Moines, until 1847.] From 1847 until 1863 he was engaged in mercantile pursuits at Agency City, where he died, August 31, 1874. He discharged all his duties as an officer and citizen with fidelity. Prior to his death, he had completed a series of valuable historical articles, entitled *Old Times*, which were published in the newspaper of his own town."   -- EVANS

In the fall of 1837 Major Beach accompanied General Street, who conducted a party of 30 chiefs to the East, and while there they visited Boston.

"There were two theaters then in Boston, and a struggle ensued between them to obtain the presence of the Indians, in order to 'draw houses.' At the Tremont, the aristocratic and fashionable one, the famous tragedian, Forrest, was filling an engagement. His great play, in which he acted the part of a gladiator, and always drew his largest audiences, had not yet come off, and the manager was disinclined to bring it out while the Indians were there, as their presence always insured a full house. General Street, being a Presbyterian, was not much in the theatrical line, and hence the writer, who had recently become his son-in-law, took these matters off his hands; and, as he knew this particular play would suit the Indians far better than those simple, declamatory tragedies, in which, as they could not understand a word, there was no action to keep them interested, he finally prevailed upon Mr. Barry, the manager, to bring it out, promising that all the Indians should come.

In the exciting scene were the gladiators engage in deadly combat, the Indians gazed with eager, breathless anxiety; and as Forrest, finally pierced through the breast with his adversary's sword, fell dying, and as the other drew his bloody weapon from the body, heaving in the convulsions of its expiring throes, while the curtain falls, the whole Indian company burst out with their fiercest war whoop. It was a frightful yell to strike suddenly upon unaccustomed ears, and was instantly succeeded by screams of terror from among the more nervous of the ladies and children. For an instant the audience seemed at a loss, but soon uttered a hearty round of applause – a just tribute to both actor and Indians.

After ceding the belt of country upon the Iowa side of the Mississippi, as heretofore mentioned, and having considerably increased the width of this belt by an additional cession in the treaty of 1837, the Sacs and Foxes still retained a large and most valuable portion of our State. This last treaty was negotiated with the party whose visits to Washington and other eastern cities we have just mentioned, and was concluded on the 21st day of October. This was the first treaty ever made with the Sacs and Foxes, in which the principle was incorporated that had just then begun to be adopted, of making the sum allowed the Indians for their land a permanent fund, to be held in trust by the United States, upon which interest only, at the rate of five per cent. would be annually paid to them. Hitherto it had been the custom to provide that the gross sum granted for a cession should be paid in yearly installments. For instance, $10,000 in regular payments of $1,000, over a term of ten years, would have left the Indians, at the end of that time, destitute of all further benefit from that cession. But now the more humane policy had come to be followed – of saving for them, in perpetuity, the principal sum. For their cession of 1837, they were allowed $200,000; upon which the interest annually paid is $10,000; and the treaty of October 11, 1842, that finally dispossessed them of their land in Iowa, pays them $40,000, as the interest upon $800,000, which, together with the payment by the United States of a large number of claims, and some minor stipulations

CHIEF WAPELLO

Chief Appanoose

of a cash character, was the consideration for which that cessation was obtained. Under a very old treaty, they were also receiving an unlimited annuity of $1,000, so that now there is the yearly sum of $51,000 payable to the Sac and Foxes, as long as any of their people live to claim and receive it.

This treaty of 1837 also stipulated for the erection of mills and support of millers; the breaking up and fencing of fields; the establishment of a model farm, and other schemes of the pestilent brood of so-called philanthropists who were then beginning to devise their various plans for plundering the savages, and fastening upon them their hosts of vampires and leeches, schemes causing the outlay of many thousands of dollars of the money granted to these Indians for their lands, from which, it is safe to say, they never derived the slightest benefit.

Appanoose persuaded General Street that Sugar Creek, between Ottumwa and Agency, was 50 miles long, and the General had a mill erected on it. A freshet occurred within the next twelve months or so, sufficient in size and force to wash it away; but the writer doubts if ever a bushel of grain was ground in it, nor, had it stood to this day, and had the Indians remained to this day, does he believe they could have been prevailed upon to have raised a bushel of corn to carry to it. Another mill was put up on Soap Creek, and when the writer took charge of the Agency, in June, 1840, that was also destroyed; but as that was a better stream and as he was fortunate enough to secure the services of Peter Wood, a man who fully understood his business, and was honestly disposed to attend to it, a second mill that was erected fared better, but the Indians took no interest in it whatever.

A large field, cornering where the creek just below the depot at Ottumwa debouches from the bluff, was made and cultivated for one of the villages then located opposite. The field extended in this direction and toward the river. Another was made on the opposite bank near to the villages, and still a third in the same neighborhood, giving one to each of the three villages located opposite and below Ottumwa. A splendid wheat crop, harvested by the hands employed on the Pattern Farm, was stacked and a very high fence built around until it could be threshed; but in a very little time, the young men, too lazy to hunt up their ponies if turned out to graze, and having no squaws of whom to exact the duty, tore down the fences and turned their ponies upon the grain.

Chief Keokuk

At the time of General Street's decease, the Indians were occupying their country with their permanent, or spring and summer villages, located as follows: Upon the bank of the Des Moines, opposite the mouth of Sugar Creek, where there is a quite a spacious bottom extending for a mile or more below, where the bluff closes in pretty closely upon the bank, and for a much longer distance in the up-river direction toward and past Ottumwa, was the village of Keokuk; and still above, were those of Wapello, Foxes, and Appanoose, a Sac chief. According to the writer's present memory, that of Wapello was the intermediate one. Keokuk himself had selected a pleasant, commanding and picturesque point for his own summer wigwam, some half way up the side of the bluff, in the rear of his village, where, with his own little field of corn and beans, despite the large field of Uncle Sam just beneath him, he enjoyed the *otium cum dignitate* of his authority and rank during the hot weather.

His wigwam was a very conspicuous object to a traveler along the road that crests the bluff and winds down the long hill to Sugar Creek on this side. From his elevated position, where, like another Robinson Crusoe in the boys' story books, he could contemplate himself as 'monarch of all he surveyed,' he had a fine view of the three villages spread beneath him, as well as of the bluffs and bottoms for a considerable distance up and down the river on this side. Several of the lodges in every town had their own small patches of cultivated ground in the neighborhood of their villages; but the hillside, now covered by Ottumwa, seemed to offer them more attractive spots for this purpose, probably because the soil was more easily worked, and situated more favorably for the influence of the sun than upon their side of the river. A light, easily turned soil was, of course, an object to the poor squaws upon whom devolved the duty of working it with their hoes, and of inserting the rickety posts that, with light poles bound to them, made the fence, not exceeding four feet in height, but, in general, very respectfully treated by the ponies, the only animal liable to intrude injuriously upon their fields.

The whole hillside on its lower slope, for they seldom cultivated it more than half way up, was occupied in this way by the Indians, from some distance below the depot fully up to or above the court house; often the writer, on the receipt of some instructions requiring a 'talk' with the leading men, in order to save time, and to the Indians the trouble of a

1875 map of a portion of Wapello County, showing the course of the Des Moines River and the relative positions of Agency, Cliffland, and Port Richmond (now South Ottumwa, the location where the village of Chief Appanoose is reported to have stood)

ride to Agency, has appointed some shady spot in one of these patches.

    The Indians seldom occupied their permanent villages, except during the time of planting or securing their crops, after which they would start out on a short hunt, if the annuity – which was generally paid within the six weeks from the 1st of September – had not yet been received. Immediately after payment it was their custom to leave the village for the winter, hunting through this season by families and small parties, leading the regular nomad life, changing their location from time to time as the supply of game and the need – so essential to their comfort – of seeking places near to timbered streams best protected from the rigors of weather would require."   -- BEACH

"The Sacs and Foxes were quite friendly and manageable; in fact, were very pleasant and agreeable people to live among, and all public and personal intercourse with them rolled smoothly along the well-worn track, without much of incident or marvel, until the final sale of their remaining Iowa domain. Sometimes incidents would occur, possessing excitement or amusement enough to encroach for a little upon the monotony that otherwise might have become tedious, of which the writer will endeavor to recover the memory of one or two that may amuse the reader.

The Sacs and Foxes, like all other Indians, were a very religious people, in their way, always maintaining the observance of a good many rites, ceremonies and feasts in their worship of the Kitche Mulito, or Great Spirit. Fasts did not seem to be prescribed in any of their missals, however, because, perhaps forced ones, under scarcity of game or other edibles, were not of impossible occurrence among people whose creed plainly was to let tomorrow take care of things of itself. Some of these ceremonies bore such resemblance to some of those laid down in the book of Moses as to have justified the impression among biblical students that the lost tribes of Israel might have found their way to this continent.

The writer was a witness, one delightful forenoon, in May, 1841, of a ceremony that seemed full of mystery, even to those of the Indians who took no part in celebrating it. A large lodge had been set up for the occasion on the level green, near Keokuk's village, and its sides left so entirely open that vision of the proceedings conducted within was entirely free. Close around was a circle of guards or sentinels, evidently 'in the secret,' as they were close enough to hear, but at a distance far enough to prevent eavesdropping of the low tones used within the sacred precincts. Inside of these guards was another and much larger circle of sentinels who restrained all outsiders (of whom the writer had to content himself with being one) from crossing within their line. Keokuk seemed to be the chief personage among the performers, and the performance to be designed for the exclusive benefit of one old fellow of some importance in the tribe, who was mainly distinguished from those about him by being clad in a much scantier pattern of raiment. Sometimes they would place him on his feet, and sometimes on his seat, as they powwowed and gesticulated about him. Finally, while in a sedentary position, with a large pile of blankets behind him, Keokuk approached in front, pistol in hand, apparently aimed at his forehead.

There was an explosion, quite audible to us outsiders, and a no small puff of smoke, and the old savage went over on his back in quick time, where he was covered up and left among the blankets, while a good many 'long talks' were held around and over him, until at length Keokuk, taking his hand, brought him to the sitting posture, and soon after to his feet, apparently none the worse for having been used as a target. The outside multitude of Indians gazed with marked awe throughout the entire performance, and maintained, withal, the deepest silence." --BEACH

CHIEF WAPELLO

THE PURCHASE OF IOWA

In treaties made between the United States and the Sac and Fox tribes in 1804, 1824, 1830, 1832, and 1837, the tribes ceded sections of their land in Illinois, Wisconsin, Missouri, and portions of Iowa. On October 11, 1842, on a site near the Indian Agency, tribal chiefs agreed to the sale of the rest of their Iowa lands in an agreement known as "The New Purchase."

"... the confederated tribes of Sacs and Foxes ceded to the United States, forever, all the lands west of the Mississippi River to which they have any title or claim, or in which they have any interest whatever, reserving the right to occupy for the term of three years from the time of signing this treaty, all that part of the land hereby ceded which lies west of a line running due north and south from the painted, or red, rocks, on the White Breast fork of the Des Moines River, which rocks will be found about eight miles, when reduced to a straight line, from the junction of the White Breast and Des Moines.

For this cession the United States agreed to pay annually an interest of 5 per centum upon the sum of $800,000 and to pay creditors of the Indians the sum of $258,566.34, also to assign to them a tract of land on the Missouri River for their permanent home, also to furnish them with provisions for their subsistence while removing and for one year.

There was provision for a monument at the grave of their chief, Wapello, at their agency and near the grave of their late friend and agent, Gen. Joseph M. Street; for a grant to his (Street's) widow of 640 acres of land, which embraced their graves, the agency house and enclosures around. The treaty was signed October 11, 1842 ...

'... The President of the United States will as soon as convenient after the ratification of this treaty appoint a commissioner for the purpose and cause a line to be run north from the painted, or red rock on the White Breast, to the southern boundary of the Neutral Ground, and south from the said rocks to the northern boundary of Missouri. And will have the said line so marked and designated, that the Indians and white people may know the boundary which is to separate their possessions.'

The Indians agreed to remove to the west side of this line on or before the 1st of May, 1843, and to the new lands on the Missouri as soon as the assignment was made. Portions of the tribes were removed to Kansas in the fall of 1845 and others in 1846."

-- WATERMAN

The Indian Agency House. The date is not known.

"When General Street died, the family intended to remove his body to Prairie du Chien, Wisconsin for burial. Wapello and Keokuk requested that their friend be buried in Indian Territory, thus he was buried in the garden of the Indian Agency. When Wapello died he was buried beside his friend. In the years that followed, the graves of General Street's wife, daughter and three baby grandchildren were added to the little cemetery.

It was the request of the Indian chiefs that 640 acres of land be deeded to the Street family as part of the treaty of 1842. On that tract of land now stands Chief Wapello's Memorial Park, including grave sites, the site of the old Indian Agency, and the site of the Council which resulted in the purchase of Iowa from the Indians."

-- STERLING

Looking up Court Street in the 1860s with the old Wapello County courthouse visible in center of the frame, just to the left of Court Street. The original St. Mary's Church is at top right. The spire to the left of the courthouse is the Methodist Episcopal Church which later served as a National Guard armory. Central Park has not yet been laid out.

Right: The courthouse under construction, probably taken in 1893. Windows and the tower clock are not yet in place, and a close inspection shows that though the statue stands on the peak, the chief does not yet have his spear in hand. The fountain in the foreground, for watering horses, currently stands in the park near the Wapello County Historical Museum. The bandstand is one of several which have been a focal point of Central Park over the years. The courthouse, built of Berean sandstone, was completed in 1894 with a construction crew averaging thirty men, at a cost of $120,000 to $130,000. (Reports vary.)

The Lemberger Collection

Court-House Notice

In pursuance of the following resolution adopted by the Board of Supervisors of Wapello County, Iowa, below set out, the question of issuing the bonds of said Wapello County, Iowa, in a sum not exceeding $100,000, upon which to borrow money to secure a site for a court-house and to erect a court house thereon, will be submitted to the electors of said Wapello county, Iowa, at the next general election to be held in said county on the 3d day of November, A.D. 1891. The whole question, including the sum desired to be raised, the amount of tax desired to be levied, the rate per annum, the time of its taking effect, the form in which the question shall be taken, and all of its terms and conditions are as shown in said resolution, which is as follows:

(Copy of Resolution)

The electors of said Wapello county, Iowa, will govern themselves in accordance with the above notice.

Jno Hicks
County Auditor

Courthouse and Central Park in the snow, 1890s. Note the horse-drawn wagon at center and the trolley car on Fourth Street. Houses occupy lots which are now the courthouse parking lot on Fourth Street and the site of the former jail building on Court Street. St. Mary of the Visitation Catholic Church is at right.

Left: Notes from courthouse records setting the date of an election to determine whether bonds should be issued to secure a site and build a new courthouse. The existing courthouse, located on the corner of Fourth and Wapello, was to be torn down, and the new courthouse would occupy that site plus the site of the armory which then stood next door on Fourth Street. The election was set for November 3, 1891. The note on the left side of the page instructs County Auditor James Hicks, who signed the record, as to how to proceed with legal notice of the ballot question on election day.

CHIEF WAPELLO

View up Court Street showing the Wapello County Courthouse and surrounding area in 1899. The tower on the horizon to the left of the courthouse is old Lincoln School. A number of the houses visible in the photograph still stand, as do a few of the commercial buildings.

"The second village was Wapello's and stood near old Richmond. Wapello means 'chief'. He was a head chief of the Foxes. In a treaty signed by him, the meaning is given as 'He who is painted white.' He was short and stout in appearance and almost as gifted in speech as Keokuk. He was always in favor of peace and a friend of the whites. He had a son killed down in Jefferson county. He swam the river, traded his horse for a barrel of whisky and invited the other Indians to help him drown his sorrow. Except for his drunkenness he was a good Indian, and much liked by the whites. His favorite hunting grounds were on the Chicaqua, or Skunk River. It was while visiting there that he died. His body was taken the same day by his followers in an ox cart to the old agency, and with the usual Indian rites, was buried at sunset, by the side of his white friend and father, General Street. This was done at his own request, made long before he died. Child of the forest, what more fitting monument could he have than the three great elms that overhang his grave?" --WATERMAN, quoting an early settler

The Lemberger Collection

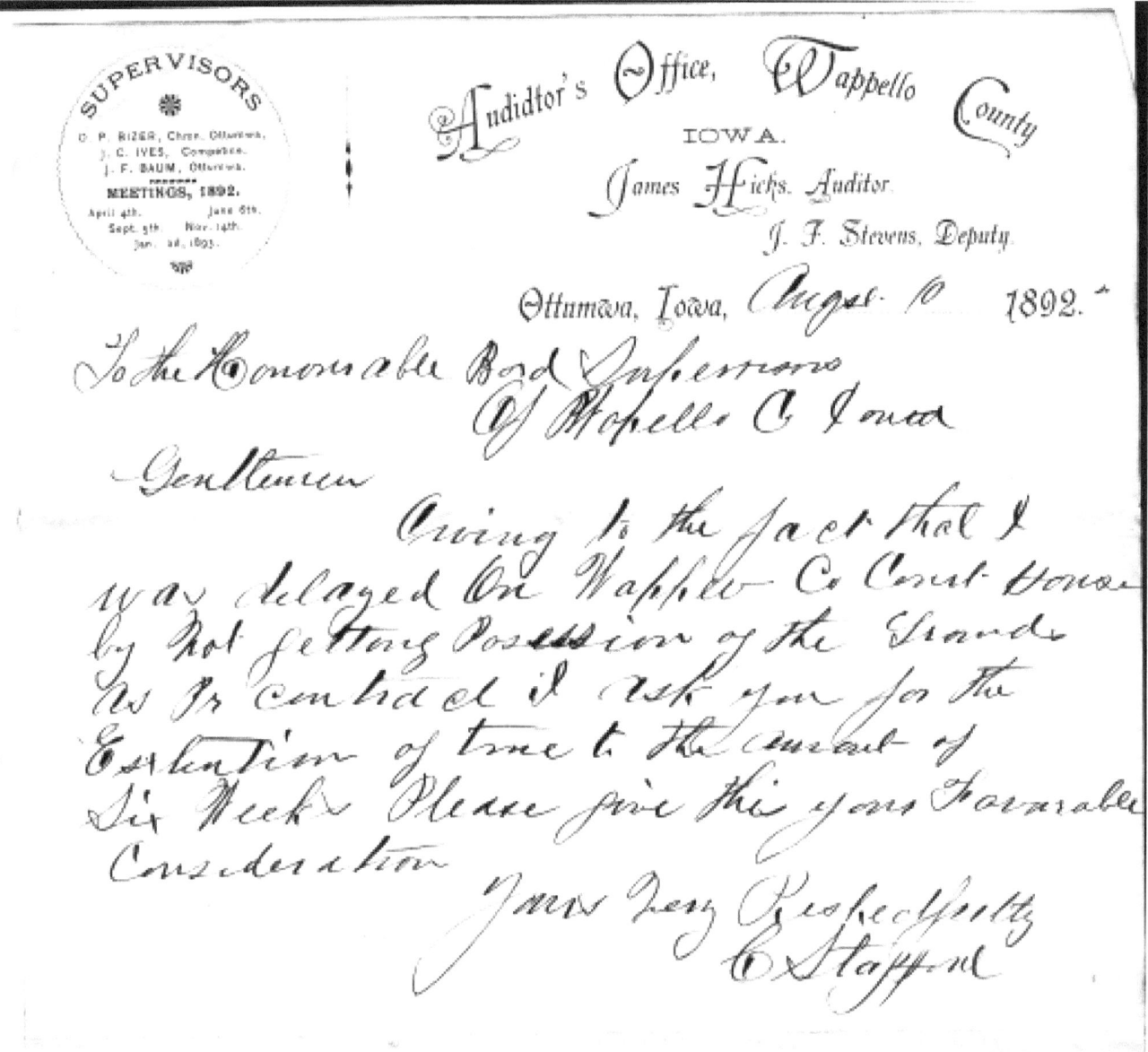

A note from contractor C. Stafford to the supervisors, asking for an extension in the contracted time for construction of the courthouse. Dated August 10, 1892, and written on the county auditor's stationery, it reads, "To the honorable Bord [sic] Supervisors Of Wapello County Iowa. Gentlemen Owing to the fact that I was delayed on Wappelo [sic] Co. Court-House by not getting Possession of the grounds as pr contract I ask you for the Esxtention [sic] of time to the amount of Six Weeks Please give this your Favorable Consideration. Yours Very Respectfully C Stafford." Note as well that "audidtor's" [sic] and "Wappello" [sic] are spelled creatively on the printed letterhead.

CHIEF WAPELLO

The cover of the catalog thought to be the source of the sheet-copper statue of a Native American chief placed atop the Wapello County Courthouse.

In this Catalogue, as in all our previous Catalogues, our prices for stamped ornaments are based on work made in stamped sheet-zinc; but now that the price of sheet-copper has declined to a point very little in excess of that of zinc, I advise and recommend, wherever possible, that the architect and cornice worker have ornaments made in copper, the latter being very much more durable and assuming a beautiful dark bronze color on exposure to the weather, and costing but a trifle in excess of that of zinc ornaments. Owing to the fact that copper ornaments are not carried in stock and must be made to special order, I can make no list price for copper ornaments, and the price must necessarily vary according to the quantity wanted, as the cost of preparing and setting dies, forces, etc., would be the same for a small as for a large number of ornaments of any particular kind, and the cost, therefore, varies accordingly.

Terms, net cash. Always give full and complete shipping directions, and thus save delays. State with every order whether you want goods sent by freight or express.

Above: A description from the W. H. Mullins catalog seems to indicate that sheet-copper statues like the chief were made to order. "Chief Wapello" was probably Indian #4761.

Left: Courthouse at about the time it was completed. The building was dedicated in 1894.

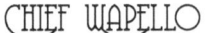

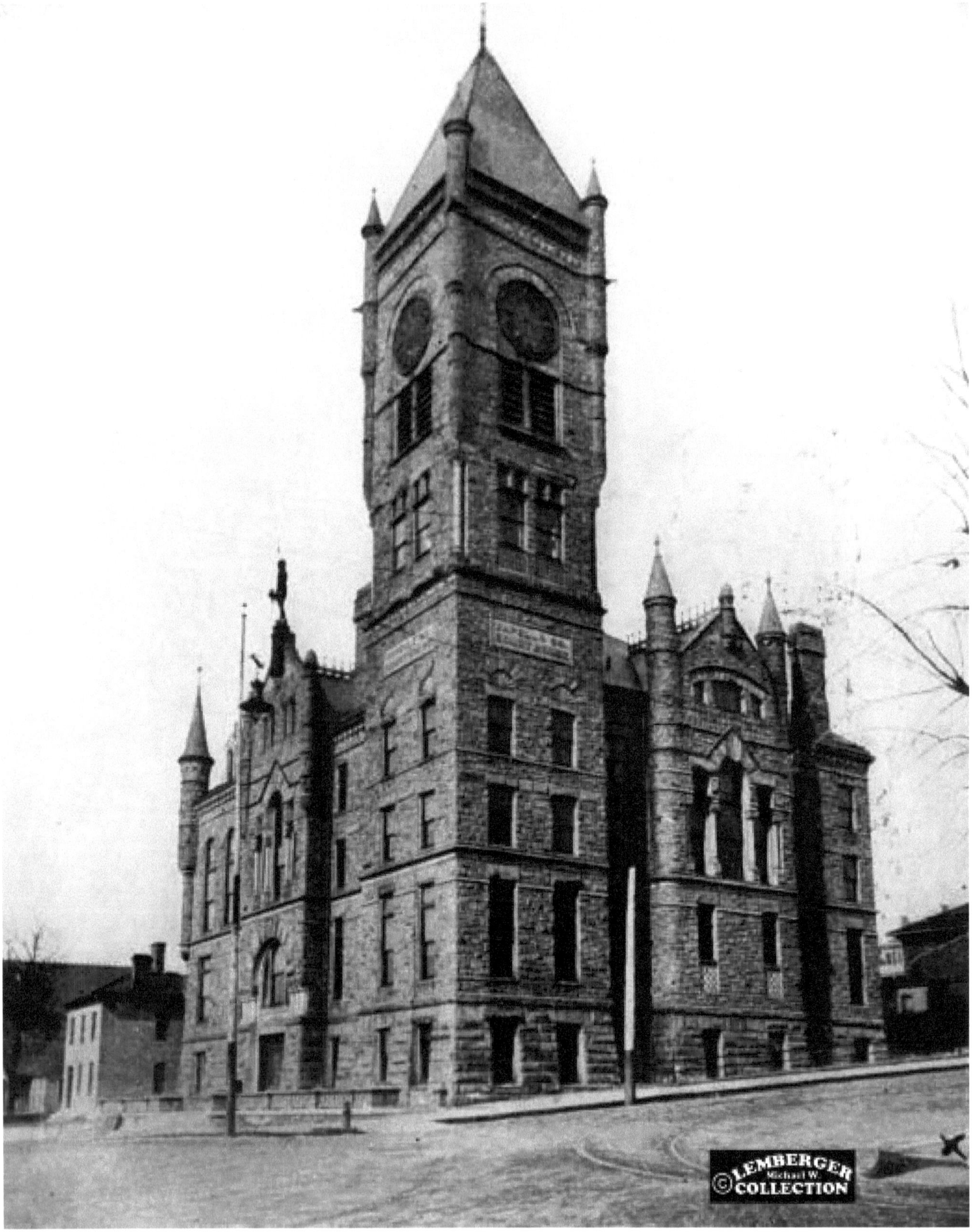
©LEMBERGER
Michael W.
COLLECTION

Court Street in 1912, looking from the intersection of Court and Main Streets toward the Wapello County Courthouse. The statue is barely visible just above the Central Park trees. Though most of these buildings are now gone, the one on the corner of Second and Court ~ appearing directly beneath the statue in this image ~ still stands. The street appears to be dirt.

Left: Wapello County Courthouse in 1907. Note the trolley tracks which run down Court Street and turn onto Fourth Street.

Agency House. The Sac and Fox Indian Agency was built in 1838 under the supervision of General Joseph M. Street. Later used as a private home, it was torn down in 1912. The date this photograph was taken is not known.

"The great length of General Street's service in the Indian department and the high consideration, both officially and personally, in which he was held, caused the department to be more liberal toward him in the sums allowed for these objects than perhaps otherwise it would have been; for besides consenting to a house quite substantial and of convenient size, they allowed him also a sum sufficient to pay for the breaking up and inclosing [sic] of a large field, quite convenient stables and other buildings attached to the domicile."
-- WATERMAN

The gravesite of Chief Wapello and General Joseph M. Street, located in the garden of the Agency House. This photo is thought to have been taken in 1895. The last of the four large elms closest to the graves was removed in 1929. The trunk of the largest of the trees measured 25 feet in circumference and was more than four feet across. This photograph is credited to C. Shearer.

"In all negotiations Chief Wapello was the mediator, his eloquence swinging many an argument for the betterment of the stolid members of the tribes. He loved the white men -- particularly General Street. They rest today under ancient gravestones and a canopy of native elms near Agency." -- *Ottumwa Courier*, Dec. 31, 1937

An early postcard view of Chief Wapello's gravesite, taken after 1901. The C B & Q Railroad acquired title to the gravesite in 1901, along with land at the south edge of the site, so tracks could be rerouted. In about 1903, the railroad erected this white picket fence around the graves.

"The present site of the Ottumwa high school, with its commanding view of the valley, was the Indian camping ground. On the corner of Main and College streets, Wapello, the chief, pitched his tepee. The Indian council ground extended from the intersection of Fifth and Market streets down the hill to the present site of the First Methodist Church. Keokuk, another chief, had his village on the bank of the Des Moines river, opposite the mouth of Sugar Creek. Chief Appanoose's village lay a mile upstream on the present site of South Ottumwa...."   -- TAYLOR

The view of Chief Wapello's gravesite from the railroad tracks which run along the south side of the site in about 1930. In 1929 and 1930, the C B & Q's successor, the Burlington Railroad, spent $1,200 improving the park, including the sign, black fence, and obelisk shown above.

"In stature Wapello was short, but stoutly built. He was honest, intelligent, and always amicably disposed toward the whites. As a chief, and as a man, he was highly respected by both whites and Indians."   --FULTON

Improvements to the gravesite made by the Burlington Railroad in 1929 and 1930 included this black-painted fence. In addition to General Street and Chief Wapello, several members of the Street family are buried in this small cemetery, including Gen. Street's wife Eliza Maria Street, who died in 1847, their daughter Lucy Frances (Street) Beach, and several of the Streets' grandchildren. Lucy Frances was the wife of Major John Beach. She died in childbirth in 1845 at the new agency headquarters at Fort Des Moines. Her baby daughter Lucy Elizabeth Beach died a few months later and is buried near her mother. The Streets' grandsons Horace P. Street, age four months, and John B. Street, age 10 months, are also buried there.

Right: Chief Wapello's great-grandson Nokawata visits Wapello's grave in the 1930s.

The Lemberger Collection

CHIEF WAPELLO

Chief Wapello's great-grandson Nokawata standing at the grave of his famous ancestor, 1930s. The obelisk in foreground was part of the 1929-1930 renovation of the gravesite by the Burlington Northern Railroad. Nearly eight feet tall and looking like granite, it is in fact the work of a sheet metal worker in the Burlington Northern workshops. It was later replaced by a stainless steel obelisk.

"The name of our county -- Wapello -- should be pronounced as though spelled *Wapellaw*. At any rate, that is the way the Chief Wapello pronounced it, and he ought to have known... [Wapello] was the successor of Black Hawk in rank.... He was chief of the Foxes as well as of the confederated tribes of Sacs and Foxes, composed of the bands of Keokuk, Appanoose, Hardfish, Poweshiek and his own; Poweshiek succeeded him as the senior chief of the confederated tribes..."   -- *Ottumwa Courier,* Sept. 13, 1876

By 1946 the gravesite was once again delapidated. As part of Iowa's centennial celebration, another renovation was undertaken by the Burlington Railroad, including new fencing and some repairs to the gravestones. A granite boulder and bronze plaque commemorating the site of the Agency House were placed by the Elizabeth Ross chapter of the Daughters of the American Revolution (DAR). This photo may be of a Decoration Day (now Memorial Day) celebration on May 30, 1946, when the O.B. Nelson Post of the American Legion honored General Street as the "first soldier," or of the DAR's public service to dedicate the Agency House marker, held on September 17, 1946.

GRAVE OF
CHIEF WAPELLO
1/4 MILE

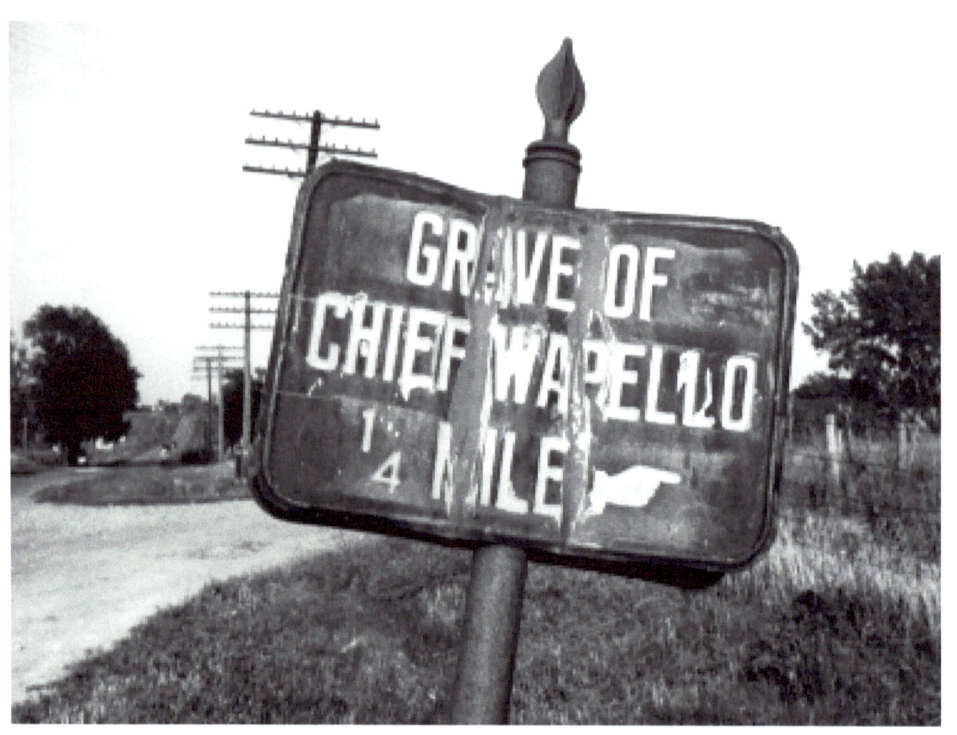

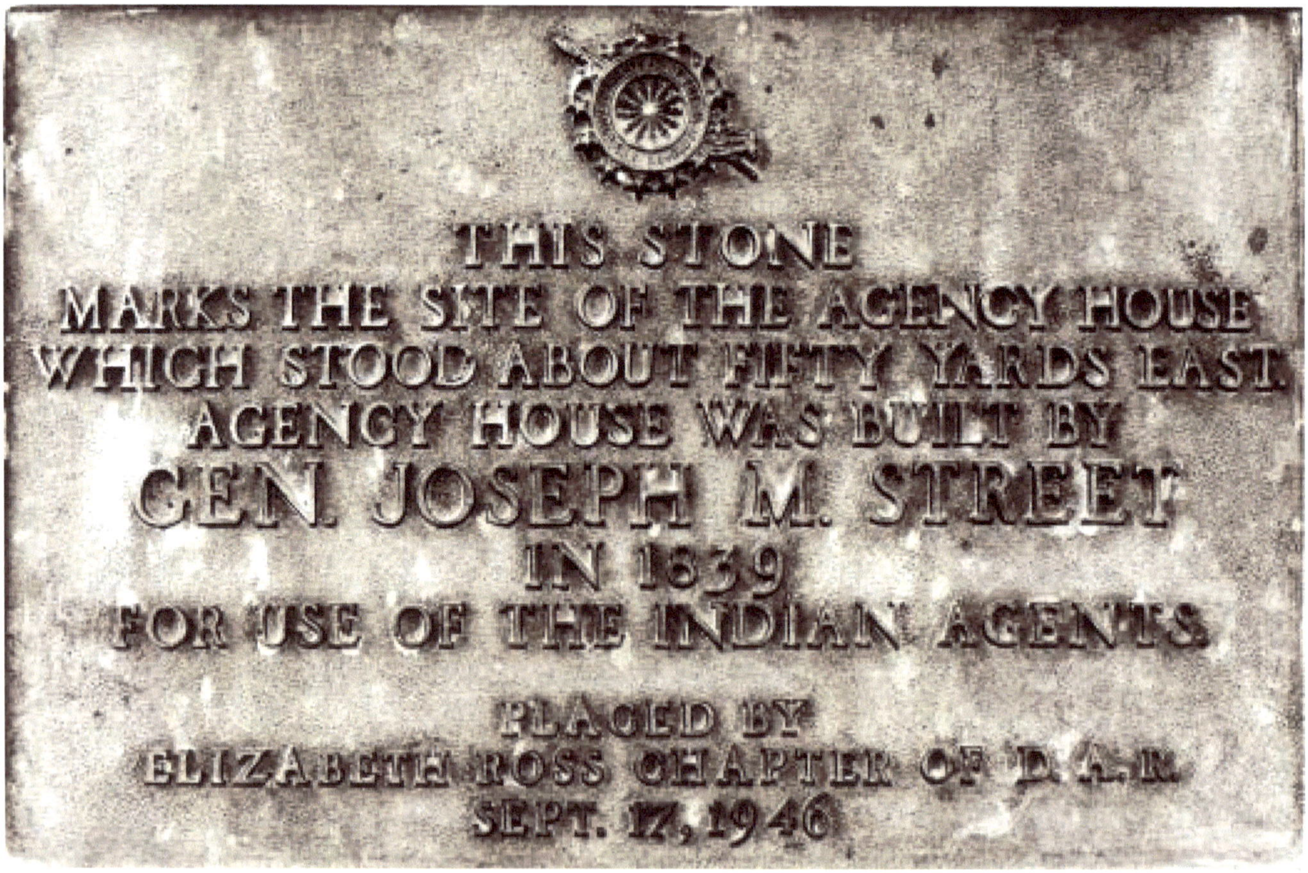
THIS STONE
MARKS THE SITE OF THE AGENCY HOUSE
WHICH STOOD ABOUT FIFTY YARDS EAST.
AGENCY HOUSE WAS BUILT BY
GEN. JOSEPH M. STREET
IN 1839
FOR USE OF THE INDIAN AGENTS
PLACED BY
ELIZABETH ROSS CHAPTER OF D.A.R.
SEPT. 17, 1946

Above: This plaque was placed in Chief Wapello Memorial Park by the Methodist Church of Agency in 1951 to commemorate the signing of the treaty for the purchase of Iowa from the Sac and Fox Indians on October 11, 1842. The plaque also commemorates the first Christian service in the interior of Iowa, held in 1838 by Methodist circuit rider Rev. Thomas M. Kirkpatrick in the wigwam of Chief Wapello, which at the time was about a quarter-mile northwest of the current gravesite and park.

Above left: Early road sign along Highway 34 giving directions to the gravesite. The date is not known.

Below left: Elizabeth Ross Chapter of the Daughters of the American Revolution (DAR) placed a plaque at the gravesite in September 1946 commemorating the Agency House. The text reads: *This stone marks the site of the Agency House which stood about fifty yards east. Agency House was built by Gen. Joseph M. Street in 1839 for use of the Indian Agents.*

Wapello County Courthouse and the surrounding area in 1928. (1) Courthouse. (2) St. Mary of the Visitation Church. (3) St. Mary's High School, which had been St. Joseph Hospital until 1926. (4) First Baptist Church. (5) Sacred Heart Catholic School. (6) Armory. (7) First Methodist Church. (8) Ottumwa Fire Department. (9) Ottumwa City Hall and police station. (10) Hall Candy Company. (11) Federal Building, later Ottumwa City Hall. (12) Central Park. (13) Iowa Steam Laundry.

Right: Looking down at the statue from the courthouse's clock tower. This view was taken July 12, 1950, shortly before the tower and many of the decorative elements were removed from the courthouse. Note the many trees lining Fourth Street.

The Lemberger Collection

In September 1950, the clock tower and much of the decorative detail were removed from the Wapello County Courthouse. The tower walls were reported to be at least four feet thick.

Above left: Work starts to remove the tower.

Above right: The statue is removed for cleaning and to avoid damage during demolition. Ottumwa Public Library is in the background.

Right: Residents get an up-close view of the Chief, nearly sixty years after he was first lifted to the courthouse roof.

The Lemberger Collection

Wapello County Supervisors (left to right) Joe Radosovich, Phil Horan, and Ralph Black, photographed in 1963 in front of the slimmed-down Wapello County Courthouse.

The courthouse as it appeared in 1965, taken from Central Park in front of Ottumwa Public Library.

CHIEF WAPELLO

Statue atop the courthouse after a snowstorm ~ January 1973.

Wapello County Courthouse, 1969. This view was taken from the roof of Ottumwa City Hall, showing Central Park and the Ottumwa Public Library at left with St. Mary of the Visitation Church at right.

Panoramic view of downtown Ottumwa and the Des Moines River from the roof of the Wapello County Courthouse, October 28, 1974. City Hall is at left. Landmarks include the Hofmann Building, Hotel Ottumwa, Market Street Bridge, and the hydro.

Statue of the Chief, silhouetted against the rising full moon in 1977. This shot, taken with a 500-mm reflex lens, is a rare conjunction of elements and not a darkroom trick.

The Lemberger Collection

Profile view of the statue atop the courthouse, taken in October 1974 from the courthouse roof.

CHIEF WAPELLO

The statue atop the courthouse is framed by the wing of the eagle on the war memorial in Central Park, in 1974.

Right: The view looking toward the west from atop the Wapello County Courthouse, October 28, 1974. Ottumwa Public Library is at center.

The Lemberger Collection

Left: Sign on old Highway 34 east of Agency directing tourists to the gravesite and park ~ before the Highway 34 / 163 bypass was built around the town.

Left: A mural painted in the 1970s shows Chief Wapello on horseback looking out aross the valley of the Des Moines River. The mural, painted on the side of a building near the intersection of River Drive and Market Street in Ottumwa, was created as part of an urban renewal and beautification project and has since been removed when the building was demolished.

Right: The Native American heritage of the area is carried on in local institutions such as Indian Hills Community College, where this sculpture by artist Christopher Bennett stands.

During World War II, a United States Navy net tender was named for Chief Wapello. The *USS Wapello* (YN-56) was built as a commercial tug. Acquired by the Navy in June 1941, she served at Pearl Harbor during the Japanese attack and was there until 1946, when she was decommissioned and returned to commercial service. She eventually sank in Miraflores Lake after being crushed by a merchant ship in a lock of the Panama Canal.

CHIEF WAPELLO

In 1975, a group of concerned citizens formed the Association for the Chief Wapello Memorial Park, seeking to preserve and improve the facility. The park was placed on the National Register of Historic Places in April 1975.

In 1976, the Burlington Northern Railroad turned over the deed to the gravesite to the group. Early improvements included repairing the gravestones, fencing and roofing the graves to protect them, enlarging the parking area, fencing the park, and setting up a display to provide visitors with information and context about the site.

The park was enlarged with the donation of land to construct a new entrance and parking lot. Work has been ongoing since 1976 to improve and maintain the park and gravesites.

Above: The protected gravestones in the small cemetery in 2007. Wapello's grave is marked by the flat stone at far right.

Right: Original gravestone of Gen. Joseph M. Street, replaced by a replica at an unknown date, after it was damaged.

Chief Wapello Memorial Park and Gravesite, August 14, 2007.

CHIEF WAPELLO

Gravestone of Chief Wapello in the Chief Wapello Memorial Park near Agency, Iowa.
*In Memory of WA PEL LO. A Principal Chief of the Foxes
Who was Born at Prairie du Chien about the year 1787.
Died near the Forks of Skunk River March 15th 1842.
And here Buried at his Own Request.
This stone was Erected by the SAC and FOX Nation.*

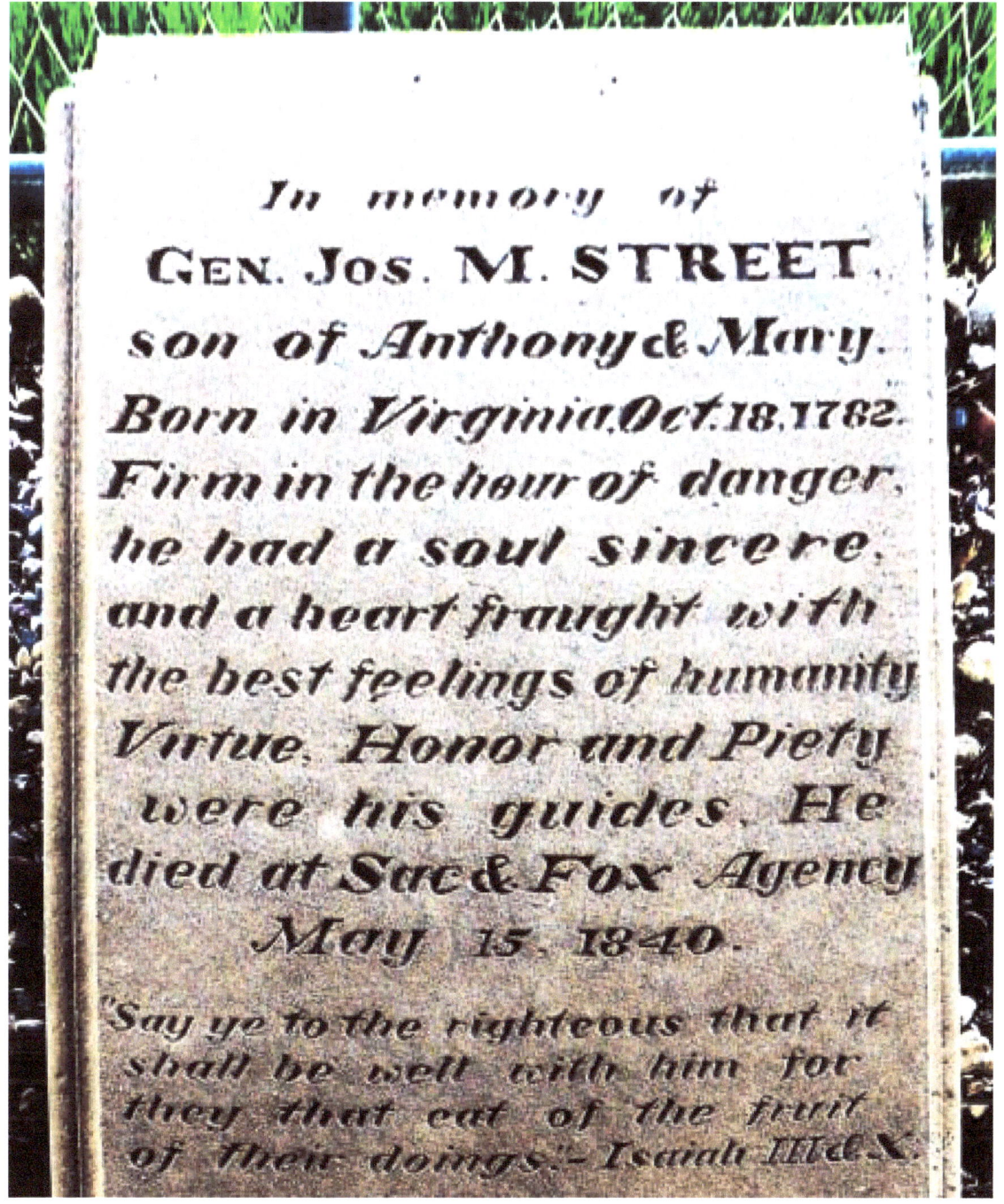

Gravestone of General Joseph Montfort Street in the Chief Wapello Memorial Park near Agency, Iowa. This stone replaced the original at an unknown date.

In memory of Gen. Jos. M. Street, son of Anthony & Mary. Born in Virginia Oct. 18, 1762. Firm in the hour of danger, he had a soul sincere, and a heart fraught with the best feelings of humanity. Virtue, Honor and Piety were his guides. He died at Sac & Fox Agency May 15, 1840. "Say ye to the righteous that it shall be well with him for they that eat of the fruit of their doings." Isaiah III & X.

Wapello County Courthouse, July 6, 2011, taken from the steps of Ottumwa Public Library, showing the Chief still in place.

Less than a year later, a freak windstorm on Saturday, June 16, 2012 twisted the statue loose from its mounting, breaking off the feet and stranding the Chief in a valley of the courthouse roof, face down, quiver crushed, spear bent. Wind gusts reached 60 miles per hour, knocking out power to thousands of residents.

CHIEF WAPELLO

The 11-foot-tall, 450-pound statue is laid on a flatbed trailer. Though the Chief still clutched his tomahawk in his right hand, his left ~ spear-holding ~ hand was ripped at the wrist, and he was broken at the waist.

Left: After inspection and consideration by county personnel, a crane gently lifts the Chief from the courthouse roof.

Wapello County Supervisors Greg Kenning (yellow shirt) and Jerry Parker (gray shirt) oversee the removal of the statue to safety on a county flat-bed trailer, as local residents watch and take photos.

Right: The Chief's pedestal atop the courthouse remained empty for 21 months, while art conservation firm Jensen Conservation in Omaha, Nebraska, restored the statue to original condition, and conservation and county workers figured out how to remount the statue. The cost was covered by the county's insurance.

The Lemberger Collection

CHIEF WAPELLO

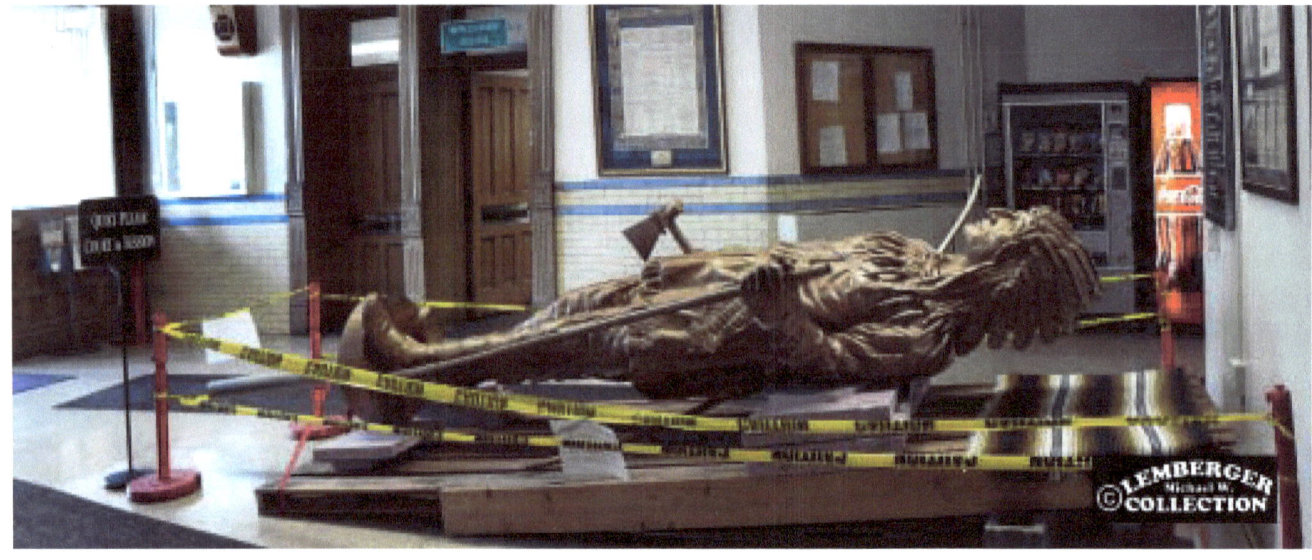

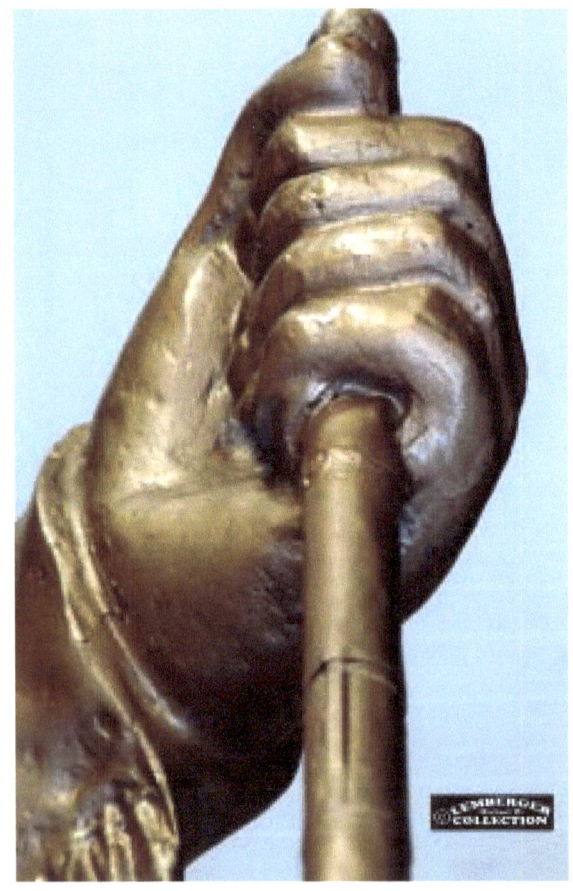

The statue was returned to Ottumwa in mid-2013, but it was displayed in the courthouse lobby until preparations could be completed atop the roof. The size of the statue meant it had to be laid down and displayed without the spear, which slips into the tube in the left hand.
The copper tone will likely darken as the statue is once more exposed to the elements.

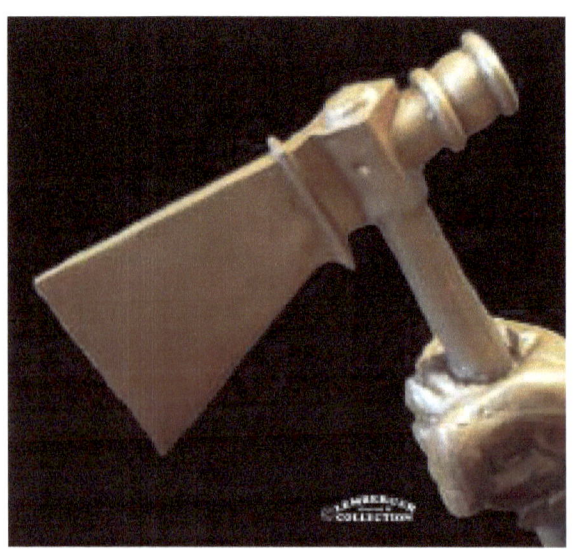

The Lemberger Collection

CHIEF WAPELLO

Closeup views of the Chief, taken while he was on display in the courthouse lobby.

The Lemberger Collection

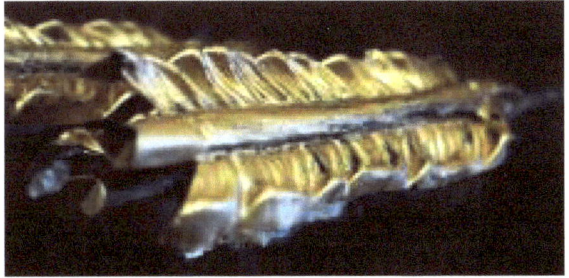

Above: Feather fletching on arrows.

Right: Feathers on the bonnet.

Below: Bear claws around the neck.

Below right: Knife and sheath.

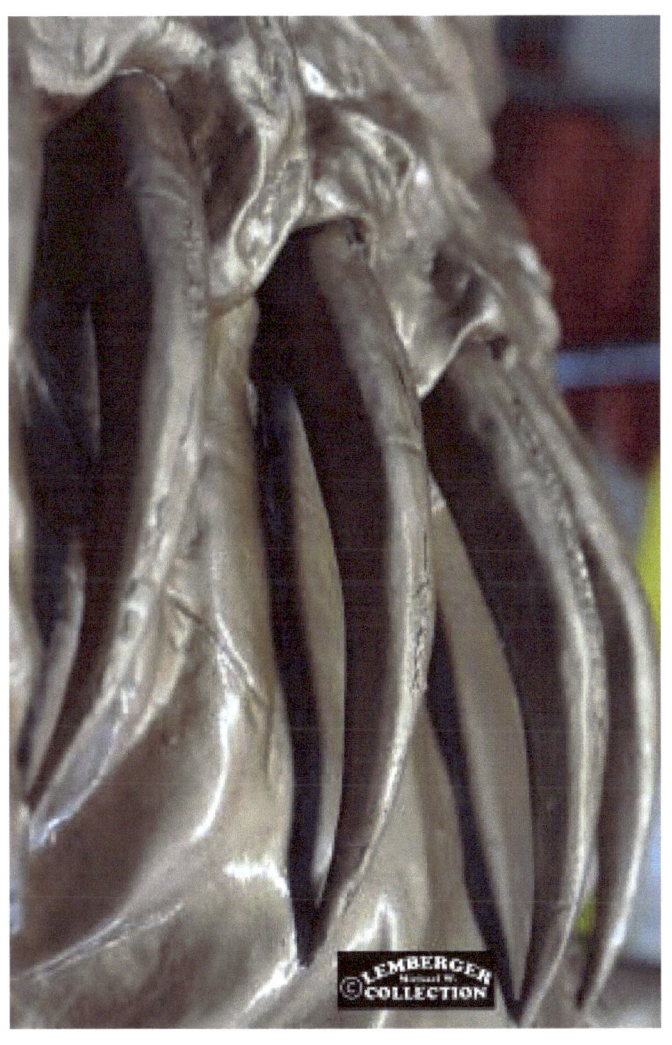

Wapello County Supervisors (left to right) Steve Siegel, Jerry Parker, and Greg Kenning pose with the Chief in the lobby of the Wapello County Courthouse, July 3, 2013.

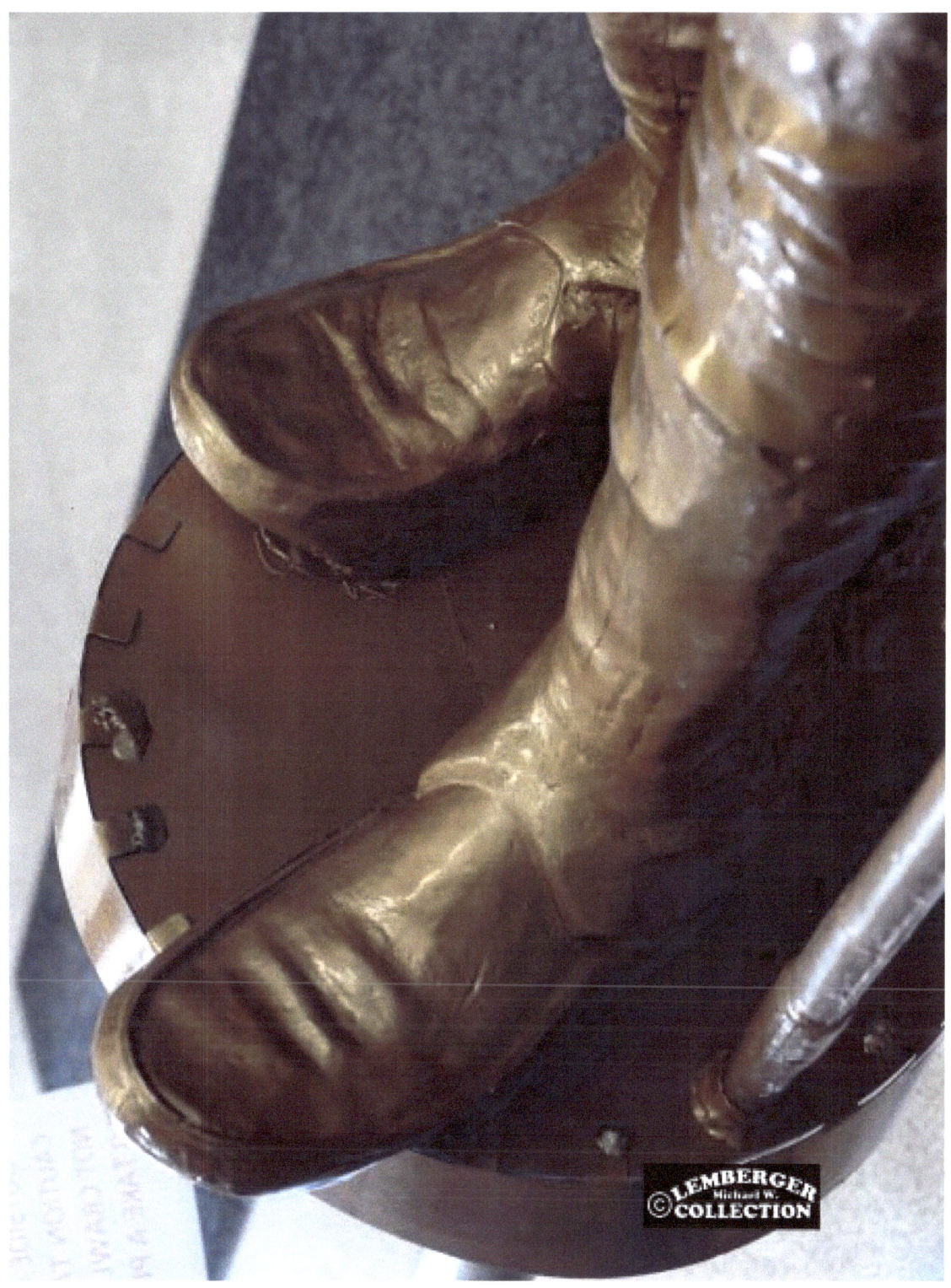

A rare view of the Chief's feet, from an angle few will see again.

The Chief Wapello sign at Chief Wapello Memorial Park near Agency, visible from the Burlington Northern tracks for passengers riding Amtrak trains. The graves are behind the tree, between the sign and the boulder marking the treaty signing.

Views at the gravesite, June 28, 2013.

The graves, protected by fence and roof. The closest flat stone is that of Mrs. Street. The center flat stone marks General Street's grave, with Wapello's grave at his left, marked by the farthest flat stone. Upright stones mark other burials.

View of the park and gravesite from the parking lot, showing the railroad tracks.

CHIEF WAPELLO

The city of Agency honors its native son Chief Wapello with this welcome sign. March, 2014.

Left: Chief Wapello, in a chainsaw sculpture on display at Bridge View Center, Ottumwa.

After 21 months on the ground, the Chief rises again on a bright and clear day, March 13, 2014.

Left: Supervisors (left to right) Steve Siegel, Greg Kenning, and Jerry Parker watch as workers prepare the Chief for his ascent.

Right: The statue is first raised to the peak of the courthouse roof in a dry run, without the spear.

The Lemberger Collection

Students from nearby Seton Catholic School walked to the courthouse to observe the historic moment.

Left: Supervisor Jerry Parker takes photos.

Below: A small drone carrying a camera observes the event.

The statue is about to be set in place on the dry run.

CHIEF WAPELLO

Workers release the lifting harness from around the statue.

CHIEF WAPELLO

The new face of the statue is superimposed against the moon
in a double image.

The Chief once more stands tall and proud atop the Wapello County Courthouse, looking out across the Des Moines River valley.

CHIEF WAPELLO

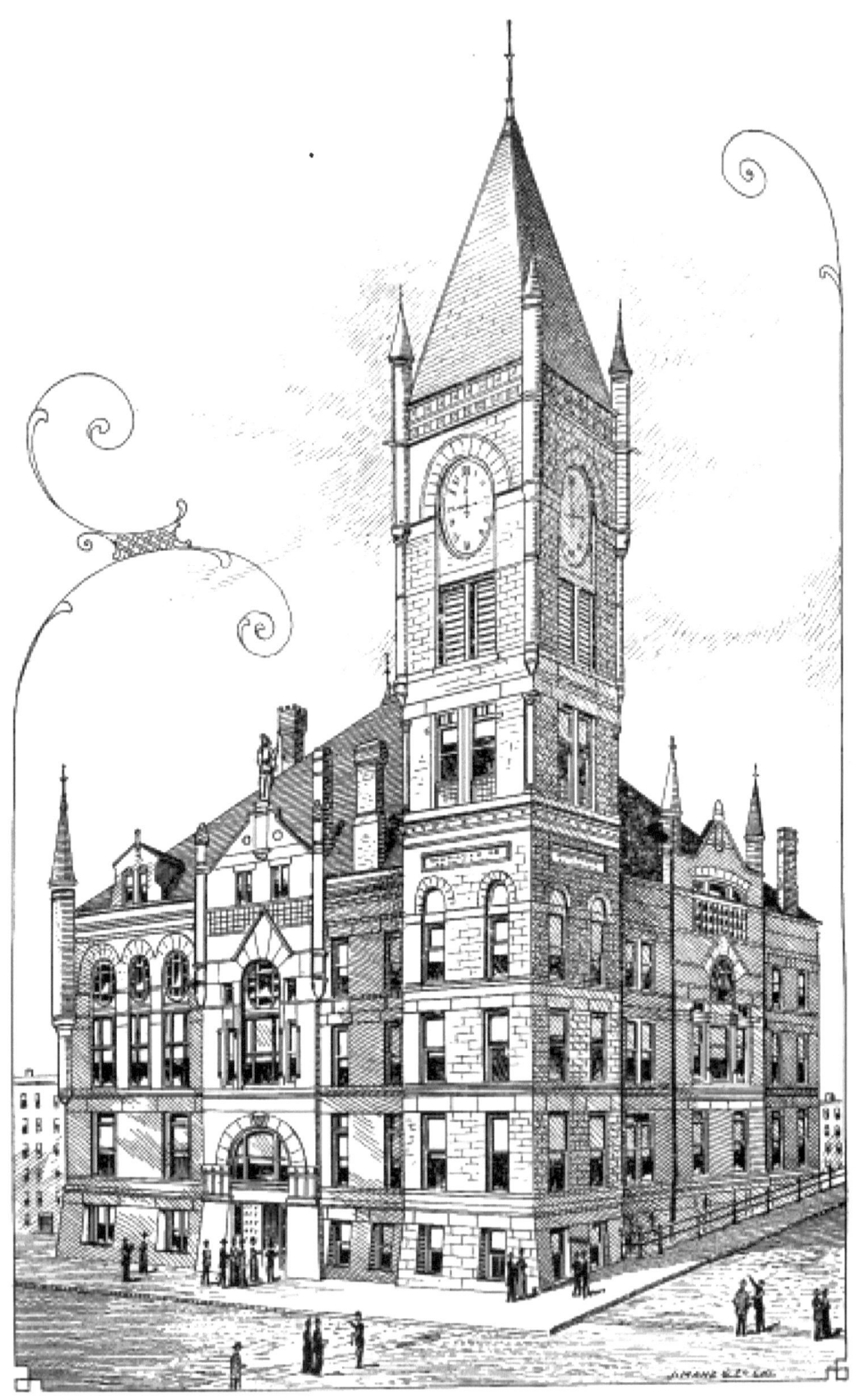

WAPELLO COUNTY'S NEW $120,000 COURT HOUSE.

SOURCES

Baker, Chris D. *In Retrospect, An Illustrated History of Wapello County, Iowa.* Ottumwa Public Library, 1992.

BEACH: Beach, Major John. "Old Times" Manuscript and articles, Agency *Independent*.

Editorial, *Ottumwa Courier*, September 13, 1876.

EVANS: Evans, Capt S. B.. editor and compiler, *History of Wapello County, Iowa, and Representative Citizens.* Biographical Publishing Company, Chicago, Illinois, 1901.

FULTON: Fulton, Alexander R. *Red Men of Iowa: Being a History of the Various Aboriginal Tribes Whose Homes were in Iowa.* Mills & Company, Des Moines, Iowa, 1882.

"Grave." *Ottumwa Courier,* December 31, 1937.

The History of Wapello County Iowa. Western Historical Society, Chicago, Illinois, 1878.

Lemberger, Michael W. and Wilson J. Warren, *Ottumwa, Images of America*, Arcadia Publishing, 2006.

Krieger, Judy. "Chief Wapello: A Strong Leader." *Ottumwa Courier,* March 27, 1993.

Miller, Mary Beth. Letter to the editor. *Ottumwa Courier,* May 27, 1994.

Munson, Kyle. "Toppled Chief Wapello the talk of the town" DesMoinesRegister.com, June 27, 2012.

Parrish, Sue. Letter to the editor. *Ottumwa Courier*. June 29, 1994.

STERLING: Sterling, Ruth. *Wapello County History*. Wapello History Committee, circa 1984.

TAYLOR: Taylor, James C., Jr., *One Hundred Years a City*. Ottumwa Chamber of Commerce, 1948.

Trembly, W.C. *The History of Chief Wapello's Memorial Park.* Chief Wapello Memorial Park Association, October 1975.

USS Wapello (YN-56). Wickipedia, NavSource Online.

Wapello, Chief. Wickipedia.

"Wapello's Pride: The New Court House Finished." *Ottumwa Daily Courier,* March 17, 1894.

WATERMAN: Waterman, Harrison L., Supervising Editor. *History of Wapello County, Iowa,* Volume 1. S. J. Clarke Publishing Company, Chicago, Illinois, 1914.

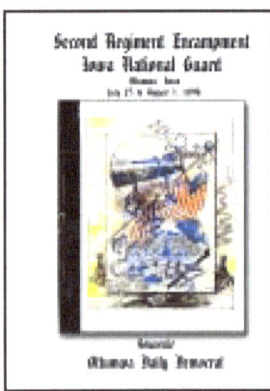  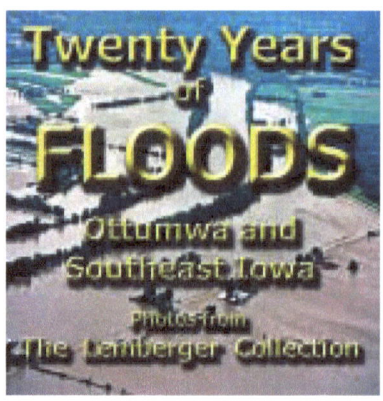 

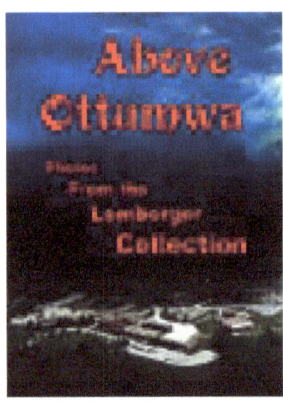

For more information about these and other books, calendars and products, visit
www.pbllimited.com
PBL Limited
P.O. Box 935
Ottumwa Iowa 52501

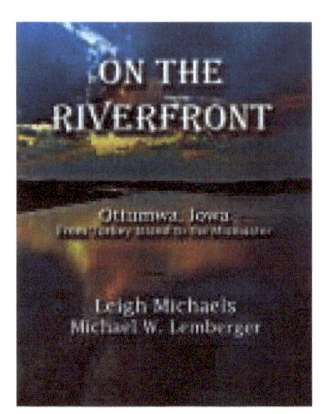

  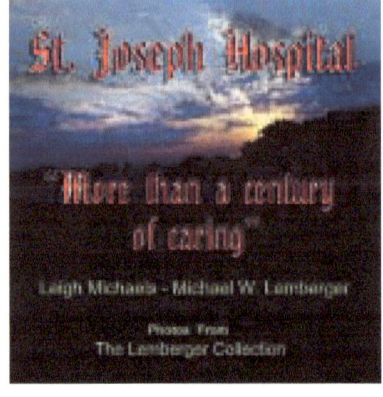

www.ingramcontent.com/pod-product-compliance
Lightning Source LLC
Chambersburg PA
CBHW040059160426
43193CB00002B/24